Maurice Thompson, Bruce Rogers

Songs of Fair Weather

Maurice Thompson, Bruce Rogers

Songs of Fair Weather

ISBN/EAN: 9783337343460

Printed in Europe, USA, Canada, Australia, Japan

Cover: Foto ©Thomas Meinert / pixelio.de

More available books at **www.hansebooks.com**

Songs of Fair Weather

By MAURICE THOMPSON

BOSTON
JAMES R. OSGOOD AND COMPANY
1883

CONTENTS.

	PAGE
PROEM	1
A Prelude	3
The Archer	5
The Death of the White Heron	7
A Flight Shot	14
The Fawn	17
The Blue Heron	21
The Bluebird	23
The Wabash	26
Okechobee	27
Dropping Corn	29
The Morning Hills	31
At the Window	34
November	36
Between the Poppy and the Rose	38
Solace	41
Atalanta	43
Ceres	45

CONTENTS.

	PAGE
Aoede	47
Diana	50
Garden Statues	53
In the Haunts of Bass and Bream	58
A Morning Sail	69
Wild Honey	71
The Tulip	74
Written on a Fly-leaf of Theocritus	76
Eos	77
Twilight	79
The Sentinel	81
At Night	83
In Exile	85
Before Dawn	97
Unaware	98

PROEM.

*Though I am poor, and cannot buy
The rare, time-mellowed things of Art,
God keeps an open gallery
Of glories for the poor in heart,
Whose walls are hung with grander show
Of color than old Titian knew,
With outlines Michael Angelo
Wronged in the best cartoon he drew!*

*All this is mine to have and hold:
Nor fire may burn, nor years may soil,
With ruthless trace of gathering mould,
These wonders of the Master's toil;
Nor can some restless child of Fate,
Some darkly gifted Corsican,
By red successes decorate
His Louvre from my Vatican!*

A PRELUDE.

SPIRIT that moves the sap in spring,
    When lusty male birds fight and sing,
Inform my words, and make my lines
As sweet as flowers, as strong as vines.

Let mine be the freshening power
Of rain on grass, of dew on flower;
The fertilizing song be mine,
Nut-flavored, racy, keen as wine.

Let some procreant truth exhale
From me, before my forces fail;
Or ere the ecstatic impulse go,
Let all my buds to blossoms blow.

If quick, sound seed be wanting where
The virgin soil feels sun and air,
And longs to fill a higher state,
There let my meanings germinate.

Let not my strength be spilled for naught,
But, in some fresher vessel caught,
Be blended into sweeter forms,
And fraught with purer aims and charms.

Let bloom-dust of my life be blown
To quicken hearts that flower alone;
Around my knees let scions rise
With heavenward-pointing destinies.

And when I fall, like some old tree,
And subtile change makes mould of me,
There let earth show a fertile line
Whence perfect wild-flowers leap and shine !

THE ARCHER.

THE joy is great of him who strays
   In shady woods on summer days,
With eyes alert and muscles steady,
His longbow strung, his arrows ready.

At morn he hears the woodthrush sing,
He sees the wild rose blossoming,
And on his senses, soft and low,
He feels the brook song ebb and flow.

Life is a charm, and all is good
To him who lives like Robin Hood,
Hearing ever, far and thin,
Hints of the tunes of Gamelyn.

THE ARCHER.

His greatest grief, his sharpest pain,
Is (when the days are dark with rain)
That for a season he must lie
Inert, while deer go bounding by;

Lounge in his lodge, and long and long
For Allen à Dale's delightful song,
Or smack his lips at thought of one
Drink from the friar's demijohn.

But when the sky is clear again,
He sloughs his grief, forgets his pain,
Hearing on gusts of charming weather
The low laugh of his arrow feather!

THE DEATH OF THE WHITE HERON.

CYPRESS LAKE, FLORIDA.

 PULLED my boat with even sweep
    Across light shoals and eddies deep,

Tracking the currents of the lake
From lettuce raft to weedy brake.

Across a pool death-still and dim
I saw a monster reptile swim,

And caught, far off and quickly gone,
The delicate outlines of a fawn.

Above the marshy islands flew
The green teal and the swift curlew;

The rail and dunlin drew the hem
Of lily-bonnets over them;

I saw the tufted wood-duck pass
Between the wisps of water-grass.

All round the gunwales and across
I draped my boat with Spanish moss,

And, lightly drawn from head to knee,
I hung gay air-plants over me;

Then, lurking like a savage thing
Crouching for a treacherous spring,

I stood in motionless suspense
Among the rushes green and dense.

I kept my bow half-drawn, a shaft
Set straight across the velvet haft.

Alert and vigilant, I stood
Scanning the lake, the sky, the wood.

I heard a murmur soft and sad
From water-weed to lily-pad,

And from the frondous pine did ring
The hammer of the golden-wing.

On old drift-logs the bitterns stood
Dreaming above the silent flood;

The water-turkey eyed my boat,
The hideous snake-bird coiled its throat,

And birds whose plumage shone like flame, —
Wild things grown suddenly, strangely tame, —

Lit near me; but I heeded not:
They could not tempt me to a shot.

Grown tired at length, I bent the oars
By grassy brinks and shady shores,

Through labyrinths and mysteries
Mid dusky cypress stems and knees,

Until I reached a spot I knew,
Over which each day the herons flew.

I heard a whisper sweet and keen
Flow through the fringe of rushes green,

The water saying some light thing,
The rushes gayly answering.

The wind drew faintly from the south,
Like breath blown from a sleeper's mouth,

And down its current sailing low
Came a lone heron white as snow.

He cleft with grandly spreading wing
The hazy sunshine of the spring;

Through graceful curves he swept above
The gloomy moss-hung cypress grove;

Then gliding down a long incline,
He flashed his golden eyes on mine.

Half-turned he poised himself in air,
The prize was great, the mark was fair!

I raised my bow, and steadily drew
The silken string until I knew

My trusty arrow's barbéd point
Lay on my left forefinger joint, —

Until I felt the feather seek
My ear, swift-drawn across my cheek:

Then from my fingers leapt the string
With sharp recoil and deadly ring,

Closed by a sibilant sound so shrill,
It made the very water thrill, —

Like twenty serpents bound together,
Hissed the flying arrow's feather!

A thud, a puff, a feathery ring,
A quick collapse, a quivering, —

A whirl, a headlong downward dash,
A heavy fall, a sullen plash,

And like white foam, or giant flake
Of snow, he lay upon the lake!

And of his death the rail was glad,
Strutting upon a lily-pad;

The jaunty wood-duck smiled and bowed;
The belted kingfisher laughed aloud,

Making the solemn bittern stir
Like a half-wakened slumberer;

And rasping notes of joy were heard
From gallinule and crying-bird,

The while with trebled noise did ring
The hammer of the golden-wing!

A FLIGHT SHOT.

WE were twin brothers, tall and hale,
Glad wanderers over hill and dale.

We stood within the twilight shade
Of pines that rimmed a Southern glade.

He said: "Let's settle, if we can,
Which of us is the stronger man.

"We'll try a flight shot, high and good,
Across the green glade toward the wood."

And so we bent in sheer delight
Our old yew bows with all our might.

A FLIGHT SHOT.

Our long keen shafts, drawn to the head,
Were poised a moment ere they sped.

As we leaned back a breath of air
Mingled the brown locks of our hair.

We loosed. As one our bow-cords rang,
As one away our arrows sprang.

Away they sprang; the wind of June
Thrilled to their softly whistled tune.

We watched their flight, and saw them strike
Deep in the ground slantwise alike,

So far away that they might pass
For two thin straws of broom-sedge grass!

Then arm in arm we doubting went
To find whose shaft was farthest sent,

Each fearing in his loving heart
That brother's shaft had fallen short.

But who could tell by such a plan
Which of us was the stronger man?

There at the margin of the wood,
Side by side our arrows stood,

Their red cock-feathers wing and wing,
Their amber nocks still quivering,

Their points deep-planted where they fell
An inch apart and parallel!

We clasped each other's hands; said he,
"Twin champions of the world are we!"

THE FAWN.

 LAY close down beside the river,
My bow well strung, well filled my quiver.

The god that dwells among the reeds
Sang sweetly from their tangled bredes;

The soft-tongued water murmured low,
Swinging the flag-leaves to and fro.

Beyond the river, fold on fold,
The hills gleamed through a film of gold;

The feathery osiers waved and shone
Like silver thread in tangles blown.

A bird, fire-winged, with ruby throat
Down the slow, drowsy wind did float,

And drift and flit and stray along,
A very focal flame of song.

A white sand-isle amid the stream
Lay sleeping by its shoals of bream;

In lilied pools, alert and calm,
Great bass through lucent circles swam;

And farther, by a rushy brink,
A shadowy fawn stole down to drink

Where tall, thin birds unbalanced stood
In sandy shallows of the flood.

And what did I beside the river,
With bow well-strung and well-filled quiver?

THE FAWN.

I lay quite still with half-closed eyes,
Lapped in a dream of Paradise,

Until I heard a bow-cord ring,
And from the reeds an arrow sing.

I knew not of my brother's luck,
If well or ill his shaft had struck;

But something in his merry shout
Put my sweet summer dream to rout,

And up I sprang, with bow half-drawn,
With keen desire to slay the fawn.

But where was it? Gone like my dream!
I only heard the fish-hawk scream,

And the strong stripéd bass leap up
Beside the lily's floating cup;

THE FAWN.

I only felt the cool wind go
Across my face with steady flow;

I only saw those thin birds stand
Unbalanced on the river-sand,

Low peering at some dappled thing
In the green rushes quivering.

THE BLUE HERON.

WHERE water-grass grows overgreen
    On damp cool flats by gentle streams,
Still as a ghost and sad of mien,
    With half-closed eyes the heron dreams.

Above him in the sycamore
    The flicker beats a dull tattoo;
Through papaw groves the soft airs pour
    Gold dust of blooms and fragrance new.

And from the thorn it loves so well,
    The oriole flings out its strong,
Sharp lay, wrought in the crucible
    Of its flame-circled soul of song.

THE BLUE HERON.

The heron nods. The charming runes
   Of Nature's music thrill his dreams;
The joys of many Mays and Junes
   Wash past him like cool summer streams.

What tranquil life, what joyful rest,
   To feel the touch of fragrant grass,
And doze like him, while tenderest
   Dream-waves across my sleep would pass!

THE BLUEBIRD.

WHEN ice is thawed and snow is gone,
    And racy sweetness floods the trees;
When snow-birds from the hedge have flown,
    And on the hive-porch swarm the bees, —
Drifting down the first warm wind
    That thrills the earliest days of spring,
The bluebird seeks our maple groves,
    And charms them into tasselling.

He sits among the delicate sprays,
    With mists of splendor round him drawn,
And through the spring's prophetic veil
    Sees summer's rich fulfilment dawn:

He sings, and his is nature's voice, —
  A gush of melody sincere
From that great fount of harmony
  Which thaws and runs when spring is here.

Short is his song, but strangely sweet
  To ears aweary of the low,
Dull tramp of Winter's sullen feet,
  Sandalled in ice and muffed in snow:
Short is his song, but through it runs
  A hint of dithyrambs yet to be, —
A sweet suggestiveness that has
  The influence of prophecy.

From childhood I have nursed a faith
  In bluebirds' songs and winds of spring:
They tell me, after frost and death
  There comes a time of blossoming;

And after snow and cutting sleet,
    The cold, stern mood of Nature yields
To tender warmth, when bare pink feet
    Of children press her greening fields.

Sing strong and clear, O bluebird dear!
    While all the land with splendor fills,
While maples gladden in the vales
    And plum-trees blossom on the hills:
Float down the wind on shining wings,
    And do thy will by grove and stream,
While through my life spring's freshness runs
    Like music through a poet's dream.

THE WABASH.

THERE is a river singing in between
   Bright fringes of papaw and sycamore,
That stir to fragrant winds on either shore,
Where tall blue herons stretch lithe necks, and
    lean
Over clear currents flowing cool and thin
Through the clean furrows of the pebbly floor.

My own glad river! Though unclassic, still
Haunted of merry gods whose pipings fill
With music all thy golden willow-brakes!
Above, the halcyon lifts his regal crest;
The tulip tree flings thee its flower-flakes,
The tall flag over thee its lances shakes:
With every charm of beauty thou art blest,
O happiest river of the happy West!

OKECHOBEE.

THY shadowy margin, O still, tropic lake,
   Is like a thought that hovers in the brain
Beyond the reach of phrase to make it plain,
Divinely sweet for its dim mystery's sake.
The real and ideal, matched so well
In yonder palm-trees and their ghosts below,
Have but a doubtful line between to tell
That from a common root they do not grow!

The delicate shifting shades that cloud the sheen
Of water too harmonious to flow,

Flit over tufts of flags and willows green,
Which feel not even the faintest summer swell.

 . . . . .

O Lake ! thy beauty inexpressible is
Except by some song-wrought antholysis !

DROPPING CORN.

PRETTY Phœbe Lane and I,
    In the soft May weather,
Barefoot down the furrows went
    Dropping corn together.

Side by side across the field
    Back and forth we hurried;
All the golden grains we dropped
    Soon the ploughshare buried.

Bluebirds on the hedges sat,
    Chirping low and billing;
"Why," thought I, " not follow suit,
    If the maid is willing!"

So I whispered, "Phœbe, dear,
   Kiss me — " "Keep on dropping!"
Called her father from the plough;
   "There's no time for stopping!"

The cord was loosed, — the moment sped;
   The golden charm was broken!
Nevermore between us two
   Word of love was spoken.

What a little slip, sometimes,
   All our hope releases!
How the merest breath of chance
   Breaks our joy in pieces!

Sorrow's cup, though often drained,
   Never lacks for filling;
And we can't get Fortune's kiss
   When the maid is willing!

THE MORNING HILLS.

I.

HE sits among the morning hills,
    His face is bright and strong;
He scans far heights, but scarcely notes
    The herdman's idle song.

He cannot brook this peaceful life
    While battle's trumpet calls;
He sees a crown for him who wins,
    A tear for him who falls.

The flowery glens and shady slopes
    Are hateful to his eyes;
Beyond the heights, beyond the storms,
    The land of promise lies.

II.

He is so old and sits so still,
   With face so weak and mild,
We know that he remembers naught
   Save when he was a child.

His fight is fought, his fame is won,
   Life's highest peak is past;
The laurel crown, the triumph-arch,
   Are worthless at the last.

The frosts of age destroy the bay, —
   The loud applause of men
Falls feebly on the palsied ears
   Of threescore years and ten.

He does not hear the voice that bears
   His name around the world;
He has no thought of great deeds done
   Where battle-tempests whirled;

But evermore he is looking back,
  Whilst memory fills and thrills
With echoes of the herdman's song
  Among the morning hills.

AT THE WINDOW.

I HEARD the woodpecker pecking,
    The bluebird tenderly sing;
I turned and looked out of my window,
    And lo, it was spring!

A breath from tropical borders,
    Just a ripple, flowed into my room,
And washed my face clean of its sadness,
    Blew my heart into bloom.

The loves I have kept for a lifetime,
    Sweet buds I have shielded from snow,
Break forth into full leaf and tassel
    When spring winds do blow.

For the sap of my life goes upward,
  Obeying the same sweet law
That waters the heart of the maple
  After a thaw.

I forget my old age and grow youthful,
  Bathing in wind-tides of spring,
When I hear the woodpecker pecking,
  The first bluebird sing.

NOVEMBER.

A HINT of slumber in the wind,
 A dreamful stir of blades and stalks,
As tenderly the twilight flows
 Down all my garden walks.

My robes of work are thrown aside,
 The odor of the grass is sweet;
The pleasure of a day well spent
 Bathes me from head to feet.

Calmly I wait the dreary change, —
 The season cutting sharp and sheer
Through the wan bowers of death that fringe
 The border of the year.

And while I muse, the fated earth
    Into a colder current dips, —
Feels winter's scourge with summer's kiss
    Still warm upon her lips.

BETWEEN THE POPPY AND THE ROSE.

HOW tired! Eight hours of racking work,
    With sharp vexations shot between!
Scant wages and few kindly words, —
    How gloomy the whole day has been!
But here is home. The garden shines,
    And over it the soft air flows;
A mist of chastened glory hangs
    Between the poppy and the rose.

The poppy red as ruby is,
    The rose pale pink, full-blown, and set
Amid the dark rich leaves that form
    The strong vine's royal coronet;

And half-way o'er from this to that,
  In a charmed focus of repose,
Two rare young faces, lit with love,
  Between the poppy and the rose.

Sweet little Jessie, two years old,
  Dear little Mamma, twenty-four,
Together in the garden walk
  While evening sun-streams round them pour.
List! Mamma murmurs baby-talk!
  Hush! Jessie's talk to laughter glows!
They both look heavenly sweet to me,
  Between the poppy and the rose.

Two flakes of sunshine in deep shade,
  Two diamonds set in rougher stone,
Two songs with harp accompaniment
  Across a houseless desert blown,—

No, nothing like this vision is;
    How deep its innocent influence goes,
Sweeter than song or power or fame,
    Between the poppy and the rose.

Between the poppy and the rose,
    A bud and blossom shining fair,
A childlike mother and a child,
    Whose own my very heart-throbs are!
Oh! life is sweet, they make it so;
    Its work is lighter than repose:
Come anything, so they bloom on
    Between the poppy and the rose.

SOLACE.

THOU art the last rose of the year,
    By gusty breezes rudely fanned:
The dying Summer holds thee fast
    In the hot hollow of her hand.

Thy face pales, as if looking back
    Into the splendor of thy past
Had thrilled thee strangely, knowing that
    This one long look must be the last.

Thine essence, that was heavenly sweet,
    Has flown upon the tricksy air:
Fate's hand is on thee; drop thy leaves,
    And go among the things that were.

Be must and mould, be trampled dust,
    Be nothing that is fair to see:
One day, at least, of glorious life
    Was thine of all eternity.

Be this a comfort: Crown and lyre
    And regal purple last not long;
Kings fall like leaves, but thy perfume
    Strays through the years like royal song.

ATALANTA.

WHEN spring grows old, and sleepy winds
    Set from the south with odors sweet,
I see my love, in green, cool groves,
    Speed down dusk aisles on shining feet.

She throws a kiss and bids me run,
    In whispers sweet as roses' breath;
I know I cannot win the race,
    And at the end, I know, is death.

But joyfully I bare my limbs,
    Anoint me with the tropic breeze,
And feel through every sinew thrill
    The vigor of Hippomenes.

O race of love ! we all have run
    Thy happy course through groves of spring,
And cared not, when at last we lost,
    For life or death, or anything !

CERES.

THE wheat was flowing ankle-deep
    Across the field from side to side ;
And, dipping in the emerald waves,
    The swallows flew in circles wide.

The sun, a moment flaring red,
    Shot level rays athwart the world,
Then quenched his fire behind the hills,
    With rosy vapors o'er him curled.

A sweet, insinuating calm, —
    A calm just one remove from sleep,
Such as a tranquil watcher feels,
    Seeing mild stars at midnight sweep

Through splendid purple deeps, and swing
   Their old, ripe clusters down the west
To where, on undiscovered hills,
   The gods have gathered them to rest, —

A calm like that hung over all
   The dusky groves, and, filtered through
The thorny hedges, touched the wheat
   Till every blade was bright with dew.

Was it a dream? We call things dreams
   When we must needs do so, or own
Belief in old, exploded myths,
   Whose very smoke has long since flown.

Was it a dream? Mine own eyes saw,
   And Ceres came across the wheat
That, like bright water, dimpled round
   The golden sandals of her feet.

AOEDE.

HER mouth is like a dewy rose
    That blows, but will not open quite;
Like flame turned down, her long hair glows
    In thin, curled currents softly bright;
Her breasts and throat are marble white.

Her lips will not have any kiss;
    They draw away, they flash a smile,—
Half bashfulness, half scorn it is,
    A silent ripple. . . . All the while
She meditates some charming wile.

Her feet below her drapery shine
    Like roses under clinging sprays,

When, late in summer, lolls the vine;
   Like flag-leaves in long August days,
To moods perverse her body sways.

Her breath is keen and sweet as nard;
   Her limbs move like a stream flowing
Among smooth stones. A lithe young pard
   Is not more quick than she to spring
To guard or capture anything.

She is a snare, a subtle lure, —
   A lily on a whirlpool's rim.
She is as dangerously pure
   As fire. . . . She revels in a dream
Wherein the daintiest fancies swim.

She feasts upon my pain, and turns
   Her pink ear up to catch my sighs,

And every word I speak. She yearns
    To see me die. . . . Her great gray eyes
Are deep as seas and over-wise.

Ah, over-wise those strange deep eyes!
    They master me, they take my breath;
In them a nameless mystery lies. . . .
    They burn with life that joy bringeth,
The gleam through shining mists of death.

DIANA.

HE had a bow of yellow horn,
Like the old moon at early morn.

She had three arrows strong and good,
Steel set in feathered cornel wood.

Like purest pearl her left breast shone
Above her kirtle's emerald zone;

Her right was bound in silk well-knit,
Lest her bow-string should sever it.

Ripe lips she had, and clear gray eyes,
And hair pure gold blown hoiden-wise

Across her face like shining mist
That with dawn's flush is faintly kissed.

Her limbs ! how matched and round and fine !
How free like song ! how strong like wine !

And, timed to music wild and sweet,
How swift her silver-sandalled feet !

Single of heart and strong of hand,
Wind-like she wandered through the land.

No man (or king or lord or churl)
Dared whisper love to that fair girl.

And woe to him who came upon
Her nude, at bath, like Acteon !

So dire his fate that one who heard
The flutter of a bathing bird,

What time he crossed a breezy wood,
Felt sudden quickening of his blood;

Cast one swift look, then ran away
Far through the green, thick groves of May;

Afeard, lest down the wind of spring
He 'd hear an arrow whispering!

GARDEN STATUES.

I.

EROS.

 NAKED baby Love among the roses,
    Watching with laughing gray-green eyes for me,
Who says that thou art blind? Who hides from thee?
Who is it in his foolishness supposes
That ever a bandage round thy sweet face closes
Thicker than gauze? I know that thou canst see!
Thy glances are more swift and far more sure
To reach their goal than any missile is,
Except that one which never yet did miss,

Whose slightest puncture not even Death can
   cure,
Whose stroke divides the heart with such a
   bliss
As even the strongest trembles to endure, —
Thine arrow that makes glad the saddest
   weather
With the keen rustle of its purple feather!

II.

APHRODITE.

AND thou whose tresses like straw-colored gold
Above the scarlet gladiole float and shine, —
Whose comely breasts, whose shoulders fair
   and fine,
Whose fathomless eyes and limbs of heavenly
   mould,
Thrill me with pains and pleasures manifold,

Racy of earth, yet full of fire divine, —
Art thou unclean as that old Paphian dream?
I know thou art not; for thou camest to me
Out of the white foam-lilies of the sea,
Out of the salt-clear fountain's clearest stream,
The embodiment of purest purity,
As healthful as the sun's directest beam,
So life-giving that up beneath thy feet,
Wherever thou goest, the grass-flowers bubble
    sweet!

III.

PSYCHE.

AND thou among the violets lying down,
With gracile limbs curled like a sleeping child's,
And dewy lips, and cheeks drawn back with
    smiles,
And bright hair wrapped about thee for a gown,
Does some implacable fate with scowl and
    frown

Weave for thy feet its dark insidious wiles?
Not so, for I have known thee from thy youth
A singer of sweet tunes and sweeter words,
To merry tinkling of soft cithern chords.
Thine is the way of happiness and truth,
And all thy movements are as swift and smooth
As through the air the strongest-flying bird's.
Infinite joy about thy presence clings,
Unspeakable hope falls from thy going wings!

IV.

PERSEPHONE.

AND thou that by the poppy bloom dost stand
Robed in the dusky garments of the south,
With slumber in thine eyes and on thy mouth,
Sandalled with silence, having in thy hand
A philter for Death and a sleep-bearing wand,
Bringest thou the immitigable fire and drouth?

No; for thy shadowy hair is full of balm,
Thy philter is delight, thy wand gives rest.
See, now I fold my hands upon my breast!
Come, touch me with thy cool and soothing
    palm,
Lull me to measureless sleep, ineffable calm,
And bear me to thy garden in the west,
Beyond whose ever-clouded confine lies
A sweet, illimitable paradise!

IN THE HAUNTS OF BASS AND BREAM.

I.

DREAMS come true, and everything
Is fresh and lusty in the spring.

In groves, that smell like ambergris,
Wind-songs, bird-songs, never cease.

Go with me down by the stream,
Haunt of bass and purple bream;

Feel the pleasure, keen and sweet,
When the cool waves lap your feet;

Catch the breath of moss and mould,
Hear the grosbeak's whistle bold;

See the heron all alone
Mid-stream on a slippery stone,

Or, on some decaying log,
Spearing snail or water-frog;

See the shoals of sun-perch shine
Among the pebbles smooth and fine,

Whilst the sprawling turtles swim
In the eddies cool and dim!

II.

The busy nuthatch climbs his tree,
Around the great bole spirally,

Peeping into wrinkles gray,
Under ruffled lichens gay,

Lazily piping one sharp note
From his silver mailèd throat;

And down the wind the catbird's song
A slender medley trails along.

Here a grackle chirping low,
There a crested vireo;

Deep in tangled underbrush
Flits the shadowy hermit-thrush;

Cooes the dove, the robin trills,
The crows caw from the airy hills;

Purple finch and pewee gray,
Blue-bird, swallow, oriole gay, —

Every tongue of Nature sings;
The air is palpitant with wings!

Halcyon prophecies come to pass
In the haunts of bream and bass.

III.

Bubble, bubble, flows the stream,
Like an old tune through a dream.

Now I cast my silken line;
See the gay lure spin and shine,

While with delicate touch I feel
The gentle pulses of the reel.

Halcyon laughs and cuckoo cries;
Through its leaves the plane-tree sighs.

Bubble, bubble, flows the stream,
Here a glow and there a gleam;

Coolness all about me creeping,
Fragrance all my senses steeping, —

Spicewood, sweet-gum, sassafras,
Calamus and water-grass,

Giving up their pungent smells,
Drawn from Nature's secret wells;

On the cool breath of the morn,
Perfume of the cock-spur thorn,

Green spathes of the dragon-root,
Indian turnip's tender shoot,

Dogwood, red-bud, elder, ash,
Snowy gleam and purple flash,

Hillside thickets, densely green,
That the partridge revels in!

IV.

I see the morning-glory's curl,
The curious star-flower's pointed whorl;

Hear the woodpecker, rap-a-tap!
See him with his cardinal's cap!

And the querulous, leering jay,
How he clamors for a fray!

Patiently I draw and cast,
Keenly expectant till, at last,

Comes a flash, down in the stream,
Never made by perch or bream;

Then a mighty weight I feel,
Sings the line and whirs the reel!

V.

Out of a giant tulip-tree
A great gay blossom falls on me;

Old gold and fire its petals are,
It flashes like a falling star.

A big blue heron flying by
Looks at me with a greedy eye.

I see a stripéd squirrel shoot
Into a hollow maple-root;

A bumble-bee with mail all rust,
His thighs puffed out with anther-dust,

Clasps a shrinking bloom about,
And draws her amber sweetness out.

VI.

Bubble, bubble, flows the stream,
Like a song heard in a dream.

A white-faced hornet hurtles by,
Lags a turquoise butterfly, —

One intent on prey and treasure,
One afloat on tides of pleasure!

Sunshine arrows, swift and keen,
Pierce the burr-oak's helmet green.

VII.

I follow where my victim leads
Through tangles of rank water-weeds,

O'er stone and root and knotty log,
O'er faithless bits of reedy bog.

I wonder will he ever stop?
The reel hums like a humming top!

Through graceful curves he sweeps the line,
He sulks, he starts, his colors shine,

Whilst I, all flushed and breathless, tear
Through lady-fern and maiden's-hair,

And in my straining fingers feel
The throbbing of the rod and reel!

A thin sandpiper, wild with fright,
Goes into ecstasies of flight;

A gaunt green bittern quits the rushes,
The yellow-throat its warbling hushes;

Bubble, bubble, flows the stream,
Like an old tune through a dream!

VIII.

At last he tires, I reel him in;
I see the glint of scale and fin.

The crinkled halos round him break,
He leaves gay bubbles in his wake.

I raise the rod, I shorten line,
And safely land him, — he is mine!

IX.

The belted halcyon laughs, the wren
Comes twittering from its brushy den;

The turtle sprawls upon its log,
I hear the booming of a frog.

Liquidamber's keen perfume,
Sweet-punk, calamus, tulip bloom;

Dancing wasp and dragon-fly,
Wood-thrush whistling tenderly;

Damp cool breath of moss and mould,
Noontide's influence manifold;

Glimpses of a cloudless sky,—
Soothe me as I resting lie.

Bubble, bubble, flows the stream,
Like low music through a dream.

A MORNING SAIL.

OUT of the bight at Augustine
   We slowly sailed away;
We saw the lily sunrise lift
   Its bloom above the bay.

Scared birds whisked past with wings aslant
   And necks outstretched before;
Some wracks hung low; I thought I heard
   A growling down the shore.

The Anastasia light went out,
   San Marco's tower sunk low;
The long coquina island flung
   Its reef across our bow.

A MORNING SAIL.

Far southward, where Matanzas shines,
    The sea-birds wheel and scream;
A roseate spoon-bill passes like
    A fancy in a dream.

We laugh and sing; — the gale is on,
    The white-caps madly run;
The sloop is caught, we shorten sail,
    We scud across the sun!

We sport with danger all the morn;
    For danger what care we?
We hear the roaring of the reef,
    The storm song of the sea!

WILD HONEY.

I.

WHERE hints of racy sap and gum
  Out of the old dark forest come;

Where birds their beaks like hammers wield,
And pith is pierced and bark is peeled;

Where the green walnut's outer rind
Gives precious bitterness to the wind, —

There lurks the sweet creative power,
As lurks the honey in the flower.

II.

A subtile effluence floats around
Where sheathéd shootlets break the ground;

And in each blossom's magic cup,
From infinite deeps a thought comes up.

III.

In winter's bud that bursts in spring,
In nut of autumn's ripening,

In acrid bulb beneath the mould,
Sleeps the elixir, strong and old,

That Rosicrucians sought in vain, —
Life that renews itself again!

IV.

What bottled perfume is so good
As fragrance of split tulip-wood?

What fabled drink of god or muse
Was rich as purple mulberry-juice?

And what school-polished gem of thought
Is like a rune from Nature caught?

V.

He is a poet strong and true
Who loves wild thyme and honey-dew;

And like a brown bee works and sings,
With morning freshness on his wings,

And a gold burden on his thighs, —
The pollen-dust of centuries!

THE TULIP.

"Caveat Regina."

SEEING, above dark spikes of green,
    Your great bold flower of gold and red,
I think of some young heathen queen
    With blazing crown upon her head, —

Some beautiful barbaric thing,
    Clothed in rich garments, emerald-zoned,
Whom simple folk, half worshipping
    And half in fear, have crowned and throned.

You will not deign to give the breeze
    The slightest nod as it goes by;
You will not move a leaf to please
    The drowsy gorgeous butterfly.

THE TULIP.

With measureless nonchalance and pride,
    You take the humming-bird's caress;
The brown melodious bee must bide
    Your haughty, arrogant wilfulness!

You will not even stoop to hear
    The whisper of the adoring grass;
The violets droop their heads in fear,
    The beetles grumble as they pass.

Beware, O queen! some day erelong
    All these may drop their fealty,
And for redress of causeless wrong
    Uprise in passionate mutiny.

Ah, then what rapturous sound of wings,
    Applauding when your throne goes down!
What cheering when the rude breeze springs,
    And whisks away your withered crown!

WRITTEN ON A FLY-LEAF OF THEOCRITUS.

THOSE were good times, in olden days,
   Of which the poet has his dreams,
When gods beset the woodland ways,
   And lay in wait by all the streams.

One could be sure of something then
   Severely simple, simply grand,
Or keenly, subtly sweet, as when
   Venus and Love went hand in hand.

Now I would give (such is my need)
   All the world's store of rhythm and rhyme
To see Pan fluting on a reed
   And with his goat-hoof keeping time!

EOS.

SHE stood between two gold pillars;
    Behind her lay a misty field,
And sunlight smote with great splendor
    Athwart her silver shield.

From her high place she shot an arrow
    That broke the slumber of the sea;
And one she shot upon a mountain,
    And one flew full at me.

Then the sea began singing, and uplifted
    Its face made glorious for a kiss;
And the mountain on its green summit
    Built fires of sacrifice.

Then her little feet, gold-sandalled,
    Stepped down the current of a breeze,
And stood upon a river flowing
    Broad like the Euphrates.

And the hills cried, " It is Eos ! "
    And the skylark soared away;
And the little fire in the east enkindled,
    Flamed into perfect day !

TWILIGHT.

SO short the time, and yet it seems so long,
    Since I last saw thee, O my Beautiful!
The very thought is resonant with song,
    And wraps my spirit in a glorious lull.

I count the hours till I shall come again :
    Each moment seems a little rose of time ;
Each gust of wind thrills gently with a strain
    Of soft, bewildering melody and rhyme.

There comes a perfume from the sunset land,
    And from the sunset vapors comes a voice ;
Some one in evening's gateway seems to stand,
    And o'er a flood of glory shout, "Rejoice !"

I seem to look through all the lapsing years,
    And see my path wind through a holy land,
While wondrous as the music of the spheres
    Is the soft murmur of time's golden sand.

I see my springs go by, a golden train;
    I see my summers with their corn and wines;
I see my autumns come and come again,
    And roar my winters through the windy pines!

THE SENTINEL.

WHAT of this Hour that passes
    With a shimmer of gold and blue?
O Love, through your crystal glasses
    What seems this Hour to you?
    I see the gold and blue
Of the beautiful thing that passes
On the wind through the summer grasses,
      But it is nothing new!

Halt! sweet Hour, I stand on guard;
    You cannot pass this way!
My heart (my master) bids me ward
    His outer court to-day;
    Stop where you are, and stay.

Your face would witch full many a guard,
But I am old and stern and hard;
   Beware, I say!

What of this bright Hour, standing
  Just out before the gate,
A passage of right demanding
  Because it groweth late?
  O Love, must I ope the gate?
See, see the bright thing standing,
Sharp, scintillant, commanding!
   Is it a Fate?

AT NIGHT.

THE moon hangs in a silver mist,
   The stars are dull and thin;
Sleep, bending low, spreads loving arms
   To fold the whole world in.
The air is like a spell; the hills
   Waver, now seen, now lost;
The pallid river wanders by
   A vast unquiet ghost.

A hornéd owl on silent wings,
   From out a cavernous place,
Speeds, like a bolt of darkness hurled
   Athwart the shimmering space

AT NIGHT.

Above the vale, from wood to wood,
And leaves no trace behind, —
Like some dark fancy flung across
A pure and peaceful mind!

IN EXILE.

I.

THE singing streams, and deep, dark wood
    Beloved of old by Robin Hood,

Lift me a voice, kiss me a hand,
To call me from this younger land.

What time by dull Floridian lakes,
What time by rivers fringed with brakes,

I blow the reed, and draw the bow,
And see my arrows hurtling go

Well sent to deer or wary hare,
Or wild-fowl hurtling down the air;

What time I lie in shady spots
On beds of wild forget-me-nots,

That fringe the fen-lands insincere
And boggy marges of the mere,

Whereon I see the heron stand,
Knee-deep in sable slush of sand, —

I think how sweet if friends should come
And tell me England calls me home.

II.

I keep good heart, and bide my time,
And blow the bubbles of my rhyme;

I wait and watch, for soon I know
In Sherwood merry horns shall blow,

And blow and blow, and folk shall come
To tell me England calls me home.

Mother of archers, then I go
Wind-blown to you with bended bow,

To stand close up by you and ask
That it be my appointed task

To sing in leal and loyal lays
Your matchless bowmen's meed of praise;

And that unchallenged I may go
Through your green woods with bended bow,—

Your woods where bowered and hidden stood
Of old the home of Robin Hood.

Ah, this were sweet, and it will come
When merry England calls me home!

III.

Perchance, long hence, it may befall,
Or soon, mayhap, or not at all,

That all my songs nowhither sent,
And all my shafts at random spent,

Will find their way to those who love
The simple force and truth thereof;

Wherefore my name shall then be rung
Across the land from tongue to tongue,

Till some who hear shall haste to come
With news that England calls me home.

I walk where spiced winds raff the blades
Of sedge-grass on the summer glades;

IN EXILE.

Through purfled braids that fringe the mere
I watch the timid tawny deer

Set its quick feet and quake and spring,
As if it heard some deadly thing,

When but a brown snipe flutters by
With rustling wing and piping cry;

I stand in some dim place at dawn,
And see across a forest lawn

The tall wild-turkeys swiftly pass
Light-footed through the dewy grass;

I shout, and wind my horn, and go
The whole morn through with bended bow,

Then on my rest I feel at noon
Sown pulvil of the blooms of June;

I live and keep no count of time,
I blow the bubbles of my rhyme :

These are my joys till friends shall come
And tell me England calls me home.

IV.

The self-yew bow was England's boast ;
She leaned upon her archer host, —

It was her very life-support
At Crécy and at Agincourt,

At Flodden and at Halidon Hill,
And fields of glory redder still !

O bows that rang at Solway Moss !
O yeomanry of Neville's Cross !

These were your victories, for by you
Breastplate and shield were cloven through;

And mailéd knights, at every joint
Sore wounded by an arrow-point,

Drew rein, turned pale, reeled in the sell,
And, bristled with arrows, gasped and fell!

O barbéd points that scratched the name
Of England on the walls of fame!

O music of the ringing cords
Set to grand songs of deeds, not words!

O yeomen! for your memory's sake,
These bubbles of my rhyme I make, —

Not rhymes of conquest stern and sad,
Or hoarse-voiced, like the Iliad,

But soft and dreamful as the sigh
Of this sweet wind that washes by, —

The while I wait for friends to come
And tell me England calls me home.

V.

I wait and wait; it would be sweet
To feel the sea beneath my feet,

And hear the breeze sing in the shrouds
Betwixt me and the white-winged clouds, —

To feel and know my heart should soon
Have its desire, its one sweet boon,

To look out on the foam-sprent waste
Through which my vessel's keel would haste,

Till on the far horizon dim
A low white line would shine and swim!

The low white line, the gleaming strand,
The pale cliffs of the Mother-land!

O God! the very thought is bliss,
The burden of my song it is,

Till over sea song-blown shall come
The news that England calls me home!

VI.

Ah, call me, England, some sweet day
When these brown locks are silver gray,

And these brown arms are shrunken small,
Unfit for deeds of strength at all;

When the swift deer shall pass me by,
Whilst all unstrung my bow shall lie,

And birds shall taunt me with the time
I wasted making foolish rhyme,

And wasted blowing in a reed
The runes of praise, the yeoman's meed,

And wasted dreaming foolish dreams
Of English woods and English streams,

Of grassy glade and queachy fen
Beloved of old by archer men,

And of the friends who would not come
To tell me England called me home.

VII.

Such words are sad: blow them away
And lose them in the leaves of May,

O wind! and leave them there to rot,
Like random arrows lost when shot;

And here, these better thoughts, take these
And blow them far across the seas,

To that old land and that old wood
Which hold the dust of Robin Hood!

Say this, low-speaking in my place:
"The last of all the archer race

"Sends this his sheaf of rhymes to those
Whose fathers bent the self-yew bows,

"And made the cloth-yard arrows ring
For merry England and her king,

"Wherever Lion Richard set
His fortune's stormy banneret!"

Say this, and then, oh, haste to come
And tell me England calls me home!

BEFORE DAWN.

A KEEN, insistent hint of dawn
    Fell from the mountain height;
A wan, uncertain gleam betrayed
    The faltering of the night.

The emphasis of silence made
    The fog above the brook
Intensely pale; the trees took on
    A haunted, haggard look.

Such quiet came, expectancy
    Filled all the earth and sky:
Time seemed to pause a little space;
    I heard a dream go by!

UNAWARE.

THERE is a song some one must sing,
   In tender tones and low,
With pink lips curled and quivering,
   And eyes with dreams aglow.

There is some one must hear the tune,
   And feel the thrilling words,
As flowers feel, in early June,
   The wings of humming-birds.

And she who sings must never learn
   What good her song has done,
Albeit the hearer slowly turn
   Him drowsily, as one

UNAWARE.

Who feels through all his being thrown
    The influence sweet and slight
Of strange, elusive perfume, blown
    Off dewy groves by night!

www.ingramcontent.com/pod-product-compliance
Lightning Source LLC
Chambersburg PA
CBHW030410170426
43202CB00010B/1550